Collected Poems

Alexander Palache Gutterman

ISBN: 9798990729322 (paperback)
ISBN: 9798990729339 (ebook)

Names: Gutterman, Alexander Palache, author.
Title: Collected Poems / Alexander Palache Gutterman
Description: New York: Rare Bird Publishing, 2024

Front cover image by Alexander Gutterman.
Book design by Rare Bird Publishing.
With a foreword by Meghan Luck.

Printed by Rare Bird Publishing in the United States of America.
First printing edition 2024.

Rare Bird Publishing
An Imprint of Secretariat Communications LLC
secretariatcommunications.com

Contents

Foreword

I met Alex at a time of transition in my life. When a new version of self, a more true version, was struggling to eke itself out. There were two of me.

One known: The past. A self reveling in destructive and comfortable behavior I'd come to know best as a person always seeking more and never finding enough of it.

One unknown: The future. A hopeful glow under which I could warm my body and feed my soul until the pulp of life seeped from every pore.

Alex's friendship invited me into a space beyond the binaries that ruled an existence. I was, and continue to be, deeply affected by his knowledge of the mystical place a person can inhabit once they accept the joy and pain of a full life. Good bad, alive dead, past future, love apathy, terror courage. His singular perception of these inevitable paradoxes is a gift to all he encounters.

In this collection of poems Alex invites you into his life. One that has provided a breadth of human experience necessary to acquire his singular perspective. He has done the noble work of living. To witness it is to watch a man emerge from the shackles of self, and so free you from yours.

Meghan Luck
Glenwood Springs, Colorado
May 2024

Introductory Note

The majority of these poems were written between the years
of 2006 and 2017. Many are unedited first drafts.

The originals are archived on two blogs: Transmission of Light
(transmissionoflight.blogspot.com) and the author's personal blog
(guttermanblog.wordpress.com).

Trailbreaking

As you know the paths about your own home
So certain facts are well-trodden
In the castle of your Mind
But life has other requirements – if you wish
You might grow outward like some plant
There are new territories, then, to traverse

Why remain on these often-strolled paths?
Physically, even the Town once removed
From yours might contain a treasure
What of unvisited courtyards of the Soul?

Strange, knowing it surveyed from the heights
They may choose instead to pretend its limits
As the fixed and binary walls of necessity

It is necessary to step from the cliff
It is also necessary to know the explosion
And to walk hours through Darkness
To break the wheel-ruts – before they become
Tracks which but faintly represent the concept of Destiny

Encounter

Who are you? Can I be certain if you beckon me?
And if so, from where? A pallid face in the core
Of a cold pond? A wild-haired child atop lightning
Scarred pinnacles? Softly speaking woman lingering
In the shade?

Why did my Soul leap when I first encountered you?

There is this strange sense that you are a Sister to me.

Proud, solitary.

Am I right that your heart
Occasionally must strain to encompass your outer
Horizons, or shorten sail in the gale of your Love?

Riddle

Just the other day, I saw them
Their arms all faced, more or less
The same direction, were slim, barren
And they danced, waving to the sky
Their colors white, ragged, brown

I knew not to disturb them
Simply to let them cross the blue
As they chose to. It was as though
I had never seen anything like them
before and had to ask: what are they?

Ghosts

You were once substantial

Without any warning you changed form
Into fog

I can put my hand through your impression
I reach for you, and come up empty

Now arrives a new question:
How to live amongst ghosts?

I then sought myself
And found only dry dust

Sprouting temporary flowers

I reached to pick the flowers
But they were gone

Diving In

You were everything unawakened in me

Is it possible, in my ancient longing for you
I was sifting through my own darkness?

Already dreaming you'd left me
Which came after you'd left me
I gave chase

While you dreamt of strangling me

(I dreamt of you again and again)

After you were gone, I was, at last
Able to tell you everything

We walked the dirt road
Looking over the bay

Where you had disappeared for a moment, swimming
While I watched from the dock

Echo-Location

Utterances are chains
Not imprisonment, but links
Comparable to action
They are feather brush, not cannon shot

If, indeed, they do affect
Then who is to say there's
Any ending? They will finally die
In a terminal implosion, or
Dissipate, woven into entropic heat
In the caverns of foamy space

If they are found hollow,
Is this error? It may be
That they enter the ear
As a bomb, lacking explosives
Might penetrate the earth
It burrows in
But is effaced in days, as the hole
Fills in completely – craterless

Some liken them to arrows;
When launched, the archer
Has no further effect. But
To me, there is only ignorance

I shout into the canyon
I don't know what becomes of the sound

Death

There was a wide, unpopulated boulevard
Simple, concrete sidewalks, black asphalt street
No cars, daytime, brilliant, several leaves
Scattered by a light breeze

I came down one side in a jacket
Unzippered, in the springtime
Hands in pockets, wind in unbrushed hair
I don't know – how old I was
Or how young

There was no end to the street
Just sun, hardness, contrast, angles
And no sound

To walk there felt good – was joyous even
I smiled slightly
While memories made themselves known to me
Though I couldn't hold them

It was my life I was examining

Everyone walks this street in the high sun
Everyone remains a mystery to themselves
Except in this instant
When what was believed dissolves completely
Into Life

Forecast Code

Just off the edge of the edge of land
I am familiar with a proud tower
The solitary occupant of which, the Monitor
when not gazing upon the frothy sea
Attends to instruments
Wind vanes, hydrometers, barometers

His is the duty to examine, to predict even
The play, the entanglement, the lovemaking
Of air masses – and the attendant results
Of said activity

Just two days ago, scarcely a heartbeat
In geologic time
A force ten gale ripped the sea to shreds
Tossing boats to the bottom – knocking men senseless
Washing them overboard
Dropping trees, whipping stoplights
Like windchimes in a monastery door

And then stopped

What followed, a lull, the withdrawing of
Extremes, difficult for the endurance of Poseidon, who delights
In storms, but requiring it. For there are a few things
Which even a Poseidon cannot master

As the candle guttered out, high above the sea
The Monitor writes in his daily logbook, the brute
Facts of the day, but he adds:

Tonight I wonder what the Front itself must apprehend
In the moment before the collision
Which creates the storm, and in which
The Front is destroyed (but the constituent air remains)

You

I woke to a shadow on the stairs – lightly treading
As dawn graciously poured itself across our room
And then came close to this fleeting shadow
Lifted her, carried her, in joy, through the dwelling
Setting her down by the table, for a meal

After which we tangled most innocently
On the bedroom floor. Fully clothed.
A thumb or finger across her forehead
Around her earlobe, was enough to rip my heart
Utterly to pieces – she does what she wants there

Have you ever?
Moving in the wide snow beside hospital bricks
She dangles a cigarette, almost tiny in dark wool
The words uncover a savage landscape, which only
Allows itself that because it is wrapped in
The bindings of humility – everything is red, and open

On the couch, it is a matter of daring. Game-theoretic self-exposure
Which at the same moment yearns for the implosion
Of the game. And, oh, if that were to occur
I guarantee you one could perish not in decades, but
The very next day, fulfilled.

Nothing left to be done.

Devotion of a Swordsman

Musashi says: when they enter in, they enter with their hands, their heads, their feet
However, their core lags behind – I know one man, downed by brain cancer
Who entered fully. When his guard was knocked down, he rested his sword to one side
Baring his breast to be cut open – bared himself – to be cut open

He died in a state hospital. His name was not given to him by his parents.

Aristotle says: friendship is possible only between equals.
Reflect on this, as images pass before you, of sunny days, of rain,
Of conversation, and of loneliness. When you call these up, mining them
For understanding, you find nothing is given.

You are a sun to them, you are a planet of theirs. This is the meaning.

I say: I am coming to it slowly. I can't say how.
Thanks to a smokeless foundry, no fire, no iron –
A singular, ghostly furnace. Cutting clumsy things
To their substance, with the insubstantial sword.

For insight.

Must be as close as possible, that contact is complete.
When it moves, it moves, advance becomes retreat,
And the opposite as well. Entering fully, doubtlessly.
(Who shuns union in the name of sanity shuns life.)

At the same time orbiting unconcerned,
As distant as a last planet in cold, elliptical remove,
The only systemic body remaining secure to the end.
(Who cannot stand aloof in the name of fear goes mad.)

In this way, somehow, fantastically, to have given everything
While remaining unscorched in the concluding supernova –
Flames lick the perihelion, but I am elsewhere.

Blooming

A realm of creatures
Vegetation lives timidly

It is not
Meadows, alpine, dotted, lightly trodden

Do you see the image of an old man
Arranging thin sticks?

No mystery
This piece-by-piece accumulation

Enjoyment: the coin's ridge
Not the ringing, collapsing pile

A drop soaks
Drowning is dry

Grasp a seed
Only view a flower

Distances

Standing on a road
A dirt road
Holding a set of keys in your hand
Turning them up – down – around a finger
Listening to the sounds

For some reason it feels "cool" to do it

It's cool out
The vegetation lowers itself
To graze the gravel
And dances around it like
A bunch of green feathers

On some guy's head in a crazy dance

Below that a curvature
Turns the road out of sight
It goes down, left, right
Up a bit rollercoastering
Down again

Until it hits a sunwarmed blacktop

Then spirals down, less relaxed
Than the stream rushing alongside it
To where its business enters something larger
But the business of the road, something smaller
A box, a hedge, a tool, a meal

Each reflecting things differently

It is 12 and a half miles to town
And 7 feet from the edge of the dirt road
To an old rock which has moss on one side
And two flowers near the other
But a horizontal, floating body
Doesn't even require a steering wheel

In the first case. Can't cover the second
Distance in the time the sun took to form
And then burn down to ashes.

Ambiguity of Passion

There are two classes of men

To one, desire is always a simile
Which names its object a dozen names
Images, papering over a fundamental blindness
Passion, an ejaculation into absolute zero
Or if, by chance, a target is struck
The child is orphaned – this is essential

The deity carries a sack of gifts
Man, regrettably, is not as fecund

In imitating the generous deity, another man
Makes no public show
As the Master counsels, makes his prayers in private
Appearing as a winter lake
A fruit's seed, which waits, and while waiting
Bears the idea of the mature fruit – requiring earth

Recklessness possibly germinates
Prudence possibly dries up

Mansions

I - Town

There is One town I have been in
One town Only
You've only made One town
I'm lost in the streets

There is One force patrolling town
There is One group of merchants
One bank, One church
One river, One School

There is One park
Where leaves are currently falling
Cut down, as Yagyu tells us
By the judgment of Nature

Why do I so love these empty streets
That have only yielded a $5 bill
When I bent down
As though it too had fluttered

From heaven like a leaf
Of Gold?

II - Mansions

In this corner under this curving lamp
Around this green Way
I also was doubly lost
In the corridors of a Mansion

Of which there are Many
I told myself there was a Heart
Somewhere in there, in those cold walls
A golden Heart that I could

Place in my chest and skip out
The red hewn Doors with their close
Inscriptions. This luxury is Hell.
I still believe that by walking through its antisepsis

There will be a stone step into repeating
Corridors that stretch
Toward the Limit of things
And I will be forever Free.

Falling

sigh down into a pile of leaves and let their golden arms cover you
fall backward onto a mattress with your tangled love
release everything over the edge of the cliff and the pile behind
will be thought a suicide – disappear into fluid

breathe out – breathe out – there is no lack even in hunger
when you learn how to dine in obscure corners
unknown friends come and smile at you
in places that no one has been before

my Brother is just around the corner
I sense him next to me, or through plexiglass
or on the other side of a Door
can you see the light streaming through the cracks

nothing to clutch, no air whistling past
just descending – expecting impact
when only earth that forever sustains
this fleeting theatre is rising to meet me – a soft landing

you iii

who can lie anymore?

no one gave me what you gave me
no one ever did

my hand is on your ivory neck
you're under me

in your graceful self
my strength is rekindled – you're a fountain

only a liar struts

a man who holds a treasure like you
can't boast of it – should quietly nourish it

the last train left the station with you standing there
at the back window in the last car

what was i doing while it left
i had the ticket in my pocket – the trip was going to be

the greatest adventure of my life

now i hear the whistle from down a mist-filled valley
that train is gone

i fondle the ticket in my coat

and my body disappears into the afternoon grey
cold, mist – i'm disappearing into a dream

at night behind the shutters of my eyes
i turn with you and will forever

Fragments – You 4

Her face in the film – she pulled off her helmet
She broke Evil
Her face became her face, became Her face
And then I knew I contained Her
She contained me

That's too abstract

She touched me when she was dancing
Like a dervish before
She went back into the Hospital
Before she fell down the stairs
Before I engulfed her and as I consumed her
She cut me in Two

And she told me I was in Danger

A danger I brought on myself – due to Evil

She was and is that way
Drawn by a magnet you can't feel – you're not
Polarized that way – and she's All Gone

You can lie beside her, I did, when she faces the Cold
And the whole room becomes Ice – I saw it
Strong Men break and run – it's what She's been given

To battle with – and no Helmet either

She touched me, she looked into and through me
And told me something Exact – she cut right through me

I've been walking where we used to walk – the world is fragments
It's difficult to superimpose this Place
Where I am smiling and a child and hold her Silver
And my Gold all Commingled
With that Self she imputed to me

After selecting only the garbage from my mixed motives
And affixing the cutting laser of hatred to it

However, I am grateful for the burning if
The burning is purification

I would return for a simple hour to the Myth
In which we entered our Love

And in the armor of hard-won Integrity
Transparent over my Nakedness

Kneel and bow my head before her

For the sword cut – final
The bent kiss – blessing
But not for nothing

12/24/06

To the right side of the road
Up a rise the home is owned by the poor
I saw the clapboards there, plastic sheet
Ripped and fluttering in the breeze

Plastic toys down the gravel road
Old car, skewed windowpanes
A curling wisp of smoke from tin
On mossy roof

Inside the dank spirit smokes
And rises with what amount of heat it has left
And perhaps wrong decisions get weighed
And judged in the conditions of its life

However outside today there was a child
In shabby colored coat
But with wild hair swinging
Holding a streamer

And turning and turning in the wind

State Line

Coming across the border from Mass
into NH the fog was so thick I couldn't see the edge
of the road until NH – and then i breathed easy

dropping a friend off at Logan
on the way down we started writing
our screenplay

someone asked me to write a poem
about putting mustard on a hot dog
while driving one-handed a pink-steering-wheeled Cadillac

that briefly brought a smile to my face
i appreciate that
like i appreciate my cd playing in this laptop
which cost 18 dollars

if you're wondering how much
see the hexagram "grace" in the i ching

tree limbs were breaking from frozen rain
i stopped behind a pickup truck
someone and someone else stopped the truck
got out, and were clearing the road

i listened to some music
then drove past as they were finishing up

all the way north into darkness
all the way into night
and if you had better sight

you'd see ghosts tailing my red lights – tailing em real close

dress it up fine
life and death all around us

on the State Line

Actually

The grunting and pleading of dying men
Must be a far cry from dreams of glory

The whimpering of loneliness
Must be somewhat removed from romance

The lash and cross of integrity
Must stand some distance from a peace prize

Becoming what one actually is
Must not be the same as talking about it

Romanian

Today
I printed the picture
To carry with me
In the car

The world is burning
You are burning

As for me
I have nothing but truth
And a picture

Someone touched me
I began to bleed
I was a black pit

A gossamer shell
I was nothing at once

I could neither
Think, speak, or write

Coming in to teach
Alighting in a form that laid
Waste to my cities

Was A_____

Blocked by shadow
In the fusion of

Ten thousand suns

Finally

I understood Giacometti's sculptures

When I stretched out a hand in the sunshine

When the leaves were shaking and reflecting

Thousandfold light points

But still no one took my hand

And then, and then, I saw the thin people, crossing the blazing squares

Of their experiences

Genius

He was building and bundling things
In a cabin
Beside the stream
Through a broken window
I saw him

The stream threatened to overflow
The candle which lit his efforts
Appeared to be running out of wax
Winter coming
Things releasing a grip on life

Making something.
Machine? Sculpture?
It was not clear.

He worked for many hours
I was the spectator.

I saw
Water rising, a candle dying
Darkness climbing
Leaves falling

Straining to see inside

In the end, I thought that

The pitch black of night merged with the brilliance.

fog lights

each time

the road is born anew

last month it seemed

the fluttering falling

leaves of autumn

were fractal frames

of auburn eyes of lost lovers

who were carried from the past

into Now

by windblasts

this month

in the undersea haze of thick fog

and endless rain

SUVs from connecticut

on their way to skiing

are measured in red shift frequencies

passing the locals

and like dreams of

when i was a child

with my parents driving
from the city

to ski

now, in the fog

all the drivers are going north

to where it is cold

and the white blinding peaks

carry their eyes back

to childhood

Walls of Salt Water

Inside the curtain there is a secret chamber
And inside this chamber there is another chamber
And there is no end

Against the windowpane of my eyes
I saw a slowly cascading blur of salt water
And behind this blur – a shining vision

Of a secret chamber

Which admits me through gates
That cannot be opened by any battering ram
But a hand that parts gauze can do it

The gates are glass
But the glass melts into salt water
Salt water – the fish are moving freely

the Fish moves freely in a Circle

Outside churches the veils open

I sank to my knees on the blinding snow slope
And was crucified in a ray of sun

Adding salt water to the snow, to the earth, to the rocks
Everywhere

The chambers are opening to quiet hands
People are entering them
Sometimes alone, and at other times holding the
Hands of children, of lovers, of friends

Leaving the gift of salt water

The Decision

Every step takes him outside a new circle
Crowds are falling away
And the commodities of persons
Are returning to places of trade
The wide world splits open and reveals
The illusion of a previous order

Streets, minds, memories
Your body breathing, rising, falling
Her body shifting to place you in better

Proximity to ecstasy

The motel lights blinding on a strip
and cars, cars, cars, haunting
The poor of the boulevards in pools
Of light and in dreams

In 44 years, containing the crystalline
Glint of sun on metal in the high clouds
Under the blinding dialogue of snow, ice, and altitude
Or through blurred salt, bent low in hail

To find your way, struggling blindly
To find your way home.

To find your way Home.

Divination

First noise, and a sound of Thunder
next speech, and words in strings of Friendship
after a whisper of intimacy, with a Lover
then a still, small voice in the heart beside the Sea

Lastly, no thing, no sound
No guidance

Nothing at all
Beside the barren tree

When the Source of the Voice is lost
Who can judge whether the sounds
Come from fountains in the clouds
Or mad rushing depths of cold Oceans

Can you?

The Harvest

He casts a wide net today .....

Details initially, finding clues and directions on the secrets of the Way

In notecards, in files, and in movement, the angle of a foot, as Water rushes its courses

Then Voices, first speaking, shuttling words through the sieve of judgment

Hearing sounds and speech as streams of roaring wind tearing or moaning

Between branches in vast forests that stand somewhere, all covered with whipping snow

Actions, sins, gain, harm, generosity, coming into the threshing machines, being ground

On the floor of the shadow of a boiling sun – seen without a dream

But this is indelicate, and it misses.......

Women, far flung, brought home, so that one Woman could be born, on both sides

Of the membrane of the Self – women pressed like grapes into a Wine that becomes

A morning drink, which a footsoldier drinks, embracing his wife in a simple hut prior to Battle

And she won't see him again

The pearly outline of a body in a vision, lips tracing its smoothness, breasts, hips

Apples, rain

Bringing all Women into the home, to build a home with one of them before sunset

And ideas.......................

Ideas, and feelings, and views.

Hindu gods thundering across dusted plains in chariots with golden wheels

Mary Magdalene and Christ seated somewhere under shading bowers

Her pearly, tiny hand, grazing along the veins of His wrist, their eyes One vision

The palace door closing, in the Shadows, Buddha walks forward, just a man ready to create a World

Caravans of Mohammed, indistinct in the blaze, resting, fighting, finding Water

In the Harvest ....

The morning is grey

Chopin reaches to tug my heart out

And ahead, who can see the path?

Our Farewell

One more step, one more, and the guest will be at the door

There is an evening light on the road

I have known him for a lifetime

He is stepping through the doorway

Calling to him, he turns his head

I smile at him, saying "one more song"

He pauses by the door, leaning casually on the frame

Evening light pours across, pours through him

We listen together

When it is over, he raises a hand to me

A shadow moves on the floorboards

He steps across the threshold, into the West

And is gone

The Veil

You stand, it is the beginning of the day
You bathe, you clothe yourself
The light is pouring through the window
You take some simple nourishment

You lace your shoes
Consider a jacket, and leave it behind
You take no bag, no briefcase, nothing

You turn your back to your bookshelves
And you turn your back to your desk
You turn your back to your bed, and hearth

You step out the Doorway
into the new day

Tangles

There were children, in the wire, in the shadows
Struggling to free themselves – they sounded like birds
Their ragged bodies silhouetted on the sky, trembling like leaves

I saw her automobile parked on the street
Friday night, when Munch would paint the promenaders
In a leering white, and his Lovers would drain one

Another's blood through entanglements of hair
And Chagall would run his hand over the curves
Of the hips bumping when couples rubbed each other

While they walked down the Main street
And then at night they will fly off, groaning, shouting, sighing
Their grasping, groping bodies will grow temporary wings

During the rapture of Union. The ones who can speak
Exactly what their bodies are saying, are liberated.
Others merely grind up against one another, masturbate

Or sleep alone.

She is climbing into airy heights that are
Discernible through the autumnal shawl – a red/orange
She sits in the Theatre with her new man, her hair

Cascades over his hand, he holds her shoulder
Her breathing exhumes the tension of living with someone
Whose mind is uneasy, who is at the table with Death.

They have eaten well, they go home to rest in one another's arms
Pale limbs, like a den of pearl-snakes all entwined – relief
While the children, some of them, climb down off the wires

Men are caught in brambles, animals have found the Way through.

You'll find me walking, alone, through shadows and pools of light
hands folded
In prayer that she screams his superiority

When he enters her tonight.

Somehow I can break this cable.

The End

Bent against the wind
A man walks through a storm
Clouds whip overhead
And rain lashes out

Into his garments
Which are slick with cold
And shine with his form
As he walks, and walks

Through an empty land
The sound of his feet
On pebbles, on stones, on dirt
He moves through the countryside

In occasional flashes
The arms of trees raise
Barren to a pale sky
And explosions of thunder

Shiver them

Hills ahead, and deep canyons
The rushing of rivers
Narrow high passes
Caverns, meadows, deep forests, plains

Even empty and barren tracts

See him in a blazing sun, under some shadow?

And see Yourself, seeing him
And see yourself arranging the home
Which lies at the end of the road
See yourself cooking, and building a fire
And putting fresh linens

On the bed you intend to share with Him

In The Body

I trust myself – that explains
Why I can walk through forests

I trust myself
Which is why I can speak my mind

And why I can remain silent

I trust myself
That explains why the noise
From today

Will never catch me

I trust myself
And that explains

Why I trust you

Taoism

I saw a woman in a jacket
She wore a pair of new glasses
But she could not match them

Then came a man in a baseball hat
And a sweatshirt
Who was drinking coffee

After that, an attorney
Who keeps copies of Loeb's classical library
Outside his office, for those who wait

There's a man
In the checkered coat
That is worn by hunters in Maine

And I remember one greater than these
Whose effectiveness managed
To turn things over, without

Ever divulging the artifice at all

Air

This morning walking
On the road to town
I must have been praying silently

The sound of my prayers
Went into the calls of crows
In brambles, beside the tracks

I heard them calling out
My need, my cry, their desires
All rolling into one sound

In early winter
Through the barren branches

The Knife

On the street
Pages blew from my notebook
Scattering across the road

Poems and pictures

I considered retrieving them
Then
Just let them blow away

And now they
Are all gone

Momentum

The wind is gathering
The wheat is standing
The chaff blowing away

Clouds are darkening
And piling into towers
Some are shuttering their doors

Some retreating from mountain peaks
Watching for lightning

Two roads are diverging

You will seek shelter
Or join with the coming storm

Otherwise
Expect to be lost in the darkness
And to be driven off the edge of this World

The Storm

Gathering again

Look at those men
Building towers

Look at the waves
Crossing an ocean
Growing, frothing

The storm front
Is coming together
Inside – your own body

The storm is beginning

I don't know
How long this storm

Will cover the Land

Sexuality

Strange that their grunting animality
Is unmentioned
In memoir or autobiography

Given that two in ten thousand
Have mastered it and speak the
Truth about it

The couple is drawn
Into an exquisite battle
Which ends

In Death

The Trail

You left a few things behind
You left gems glittering on the sand

And I trail along behind you
I see your footsteps

Listening to the sea
Holding gems in my hand

We sat kicking our legs off the edge of the dock
We watched the sun roll down into the bay

You chose another Way

I tracked you, but your steps

Passed into the ocean
I see you standing beside me

I see you in the trees, I feel you
Under me like a butterfly

Casting gems into the sea
And turning away

The Shore

I saw your sailboat racing
From the edge of the shore
Through the froth, through the foam
Alongside the swells
To the edge of the breakwater
To the jetty, to the sandbar
Where the waves lull, and luffing

Then catching a fresh breeze
And you pull across the outer range of whitecaps
Whipped by this fresh breeze
And your red hair is flowing
And your face is shining, you hold
A bronzed tiller, standing in the hull
Of your craft and the sun is setting
And you are leaving, and I stand
On the empty shore in dusk, your
Sail finally a glimmer on the edge of the sky
Before disappearing

Farewell

Farewell, friend
Farewell, my love

Swimming in
You laid your hand on me

Walking with me
We spoke together

Flying away
You take your hand from mine

Where in the Universe
Are those things that were said
When we were crying
Either in bliss or in pain?

Into what space did they go?
What, in the end, do they really mean?

Farewell.

The light is passing behind walls
Passing into earth, passing down

So look for me someday on
Another shore.

Sacrifice

The lamb is buckling under the weight of the knife
The martyr is crumpling beneath a hail of stones
Men and women, torn by wild beasts in a desiccated arena
While crowds howl and fornicate
Cast into one another's eyes, a final moment

The look of love

A mother offers her precious child to the man in armour
Who impales it; she collapses in the dust
Masses tear the ears and eyes from apostates
While in the distance, on a cold hill of 47 crosses

The ones still alive
Before sunset, raise their bleeding faces

Looking lovingly upon you and me

End

At sunset
It disappears

Or you just put it down

You stand from the chair

Or you step back from the table

Glancing at the clock

You know
That you have to go now

On The Ridge

Three of them

You see the first one
Which is a knife edge of granite
There is wind howling across it
But you and a friend laughed
In the sunshine
With a rope between you
When you danced through the clouds on its corner

You know the second one
Which is in life, of life, is life
And where words and actions
Are the rope
Between you and your friends
And the clouds prevent, sometimes, a view
The thunder prevents sometimes
Hearing them call signals to you

And you feel the third one
A ridgeline across the grey horizon
Of your own interior wilderness
Standing, at its edge, you turn for the friend
With the rope

But there is no one there

So you wait for favorable signs to cross

•

Riding at Daybreak

Awake in the darkness before dawn
In deepest night, You listen for us
And I can assure You
We are getting our gear together
We are cleaning and holstering weapons
In the silent darkness

I can assure You
I'm standing outside the camp
And my horse is beside me
Mist from Our breath – flowing
The men and women putting feet
Into their stirrups
A sound of metal and breathing

Hold on another day, hold until the dawn

We are riding now, on our way to You
We are riding side by side
The sun is rising, there is a glow coming over
On the edge of the mountains
And I can assure You
As a storm comes across the plains
Irresistible, I am at the head of Them
And all of Us are coming

We are all together now
My sister rides
Close to me
Her red hair is flowing freely
None of us fear death now
We are coming to release You
To relieve you from your long watch
To carry the day
Once and for all

I can assure You
We are coming

Morning

The mentally ill are shuffling out
There's the woman who carries fruit boxes in a wire roller
Her long wool coat drags the ground – unpaid streetsweeper

See that guy hustling across the street
Wearing unlaced black ski boots
He yelled at a motorist last week in the same spot

Here comes what's her name in trench coat
With a crate
Of used romance books well-thumbed

Down at the bus station they're ranged out
Over benches and standing by the plate glass
Pondering G-d knows what anyway

And lastly, see the fat guy in the gazebo?
He said his last suicide attempt failed
Now he sits in the gazebo next to his wheeled suitcase

All day long

Not going anywhere anytime

Morning II

Waking
Sitting up, and sitting on the edge of the bed
Showering, putting clothes on

One man is strapping armor on
And shouldering weapons
Putting rounds in a chamber, one by one

Another is standing beside a tractor
In the light of the early sun
Preparing for a full harvest

The third, at his doorway
Scans the clouds for signs
Of a rainstorm, in the deepening grey

Step out of the doorway now
Feel the wind on your face
See rows of homes, see the twisting trees

And make your way forward

Branded

Tattoo it on my left chest over my heart
And engrave it on the hilt of the sword I am carrying
Cover it over the flag on my grave
And make it the name of every poem that I write

This is a tepid age
Someone cut away G-d, or so they thought
And left us trading commodities – trading
Commodities in the setting sun

But guess what?
She's no commodity

And love is no commodity

Change

In the upstairs room with those floorboards
An ancient farm
You opened slim arms to me

At the seaside
Surf roaring in our ears
You were beneath me

For hours you called
For me, and I for you
In the tangle of your bed

We walked by glittering streams

Not using any words to speak

I sat next to you
At the dinner
Surrounded by family

In a dress that evening
You were the body of Joy
Love shines in that body

But life changes.

Today I came down the side street and I saw
A man depositing you from your own car, and
You ran, seeing me

You ran around the corner
Thinking – I will not see you

But I saw you turn that corner
I saw him stop for you again
The two of you drove away

In this world I taste bitterness

I knew not what to do
So I overturned the teacup
Let it pour on the street, watched it pour

Tonight, with the gun on the table

I invent a story

This is it:

In the sunlit clouds of Heaven
I will once again hold Your hand

It's true in one way
And in another way

We both know it isn't

Goodbye

First I have to stop crying
That will take some time

Then I must stand up
And walk down the stairs

There I will stand
In the air of the morning

As the sun comes up
For another day, the Sun

Will shine on me

Red-haired angel
You came to cut me in two

You came to break me completely

And you did succeed

Knowledge

As I write
I can hear you panting

He's fucking you tonight

I cannot see his face
Darkness covers his face

He's fucking you now

Where once I was
Now he is

Now he is

That which I once held
Now he does

Now he does

Rest

I will lie down
And I will give up

Nothing will remain
Of anything

That once guarded my heart
And then all that will be left

Will be my body
And my love for you

Beneath all of it
Is my love for you

Which never ends

44

Standing by the stream
Looking back, seeing colored images
Looking forward, seeing darkness

Standing by the stream

Alone

The faint humming song
Is growing now

In the trees
And by rushing water

The weeping man
Moves silently, and moves

Through life and seasons
And loses himself

Across the threshold of himself
He looks out into the sky

And finds all the shells
Broken against great stones of time

The Heart

The belt moves horizontally
Watching it, grey ones shuttle
From one side to the other
And colored ones dance here and there
But although they veer left
Their position always moves right

If you step off the belt
You find a second belt, and after that
Belt opon belt
And all the belts taking all of us
Off to the far horizon and then
Looping back for the different ones

And you leap, and you leap high
Thinking, just now, I'll get off this
And just now, just by giving myself
To this, or that, or to her
I'll break down
These long grinding machines running
This thing, long-running
Machines, that don't stop

And so you tell yourself a story
A story that pleases you
About those who can lay themselves down
At the feet of another
And who can then be swallowed in the gears
Never to return again

Birth

It is coming out of my body
It is crawling out now

Its hands, though soft
Are like steel

And it cuts me open
Lays me on the threshing floor

Of memory
And cuts me completely through

From the intercourse
Of my heart and my mind

It came into being

Now, in order to be born

It is going to kill me

Untimely

You set boundaries
And sitting in the grandstand
Certainly, I applaud you

Delicately – like the crowd in England
Watching tennis

And you decide to paint something
So I speak about your work

With tact, like a professor

Then you find a job, and
In the fullness of time, a spouse

At the wedding, I smile, joining the toast

All the while, I am loving her
All the while, I am preparing myself

For the grand sacrifice

You label it madness
But when you reluctantly reach
The gates of oblivion

You understand

Liberator

She came in afraid
She was a deer, an antelope
Her fears the hunters
Of her children

So she herded them
And she covered, guarded them
And then I came
Circling, not knowing

That I was circling, uncovering
The children, and I taught her
To cut, and she cut

So then in a dream
Setting forth by my side into the night
Making use of her new-found skill
She cut evil men apart

She thanked me for this
She began to carry her sword, proudly
She grew tall, she grew proud
And began to look at me, in a different way

Until the inexorable logic of life
Which brought me to her, which uncovered her
Which killed him, caused her
To draw her sword and cut me clear down

She cut me down, and falling
I fell out of this world

Motion

It opened and out you came
You spun in joy
Until you learned how to love
Then you loved
Until you found the Lover
Then you lay together
And you made a Child

So you were three
And your meaning was one in three
And you became lost
Believing you had found yourself
In side streets where the angles
Cast favorable shadows for
The projections of Heroism

So the Lover and the Child
Stood on a windy seashore
When you grasped your tiller
Setting forth into the Sea

For centuries you sailed, finding islands
In storms, in calm, resting with strange peoples
Traversing the coasts of full
Continents, listening to the Creatures
Of the sea, and learning
The way of the starry night and its direction

Until, the voyage complete, you stepped
Again to a new shore, finding
Your Lover awaiting you in bed, arms open
Legs open, to retake you

You lay beside her, breathing the voyage
Through skin and scent, not through words

Waiting for the Child to come home

Simple

In the warm evening of April
It is uncommonly warm
And everywhere women cleave to their men
Men eye their women
In preparation for
Consummation and the Harvest of Love

At around this time
When the red clouds speak of the sun's going to bed
I see Your face, and I long for you
Maybe we could walk by the running stream
Maybe we could stop and get something to eat
Maybe I could be with you tonight

There are some things I want to say
That I couldn't say before
And now

Now I can

The Evening

The tears come at this time of night
They come as the sun drops below the horizon
When there is nowhere to go but home
That is when they come pouring down

Comprehension of Love Poetry

You think that in loss in Her
I won't find my Self
So you don't understand my poetry

You apply a psychological category
Which is like using braille
To find the rivets on the Titanic

You just missed the smokestacks

You really don't understand
My love poetry at all
So, I don't think

You understand Love either

The Waterfall

We saw the waterfall
We were sitting in the canoe
It came down to join the larger river
In an uncomplaining way

Downtown, a few branches of the river
Cut unobtrusively
Through various main streets
And carry things away dutifully

The people were meditating
As they moved, I thought of trees
And against the change of seasons
And nations, I felt an underlying current

Of water

Evening

He was busy
The entire day

He got things done
He did them well

But now
Evening is coming

And

It settles down
Tenderly, on their shoulders

They cannot fight
They are stopped in the

Fading sunlight
And they pause, taking in

The change in the light

Everyone pauses
And everything is forgiven

Before the darkness

A Bridge

I will go to sleep tonight
And fully anticipate dreaming
Perhaps standing in the middle
Of a slender bridge, spanning the stars

On the far bank, that shining one is disappearing
My left eye is tearing: jewels for her
On the near bank, her younger sister is beckoning
My right eye is tearing: gems for her

The present is a vice, is a rack, is a sweet vice
The present is a demon, an angel, is

My longing for You

In Darkness

In a dark wood you come walking
Shadows all around

And the shadows are deepening
Across the land in evening time

You are not walking
In the darkness of grief

Not covered with ashes under a leaden sky

Nor are you walking
In the darkness of fear

Not constraining yourself in imagined prisons

You are not walking
In the darkness of evil

Turning your back on simple commands

And you do not walk
In the darkness of ignorance

Because this darkness goes beyond fact and fiction

What you are walking in
Is just darkness

And all you are able to do
Is feel your way through

Children and Dreams

There are only two guides.

To the One residing in the central square,

Children speak from one side
Actually from inside
Their voices come from somewhere
Wildly sincere. Eyes
Are interested in seeing what We do
With what They request of us.

Dreams on the other hand
Are the premonitions of Unity
As that Thing which so long ago
Was shattered from Itself

Gropes uneven ground, sliding Pieces
of Itself against Itself. Until

Its hands glide across smoothness.

Trembling

Lying on his back, he sees
Branches arcing to the white blank sky

Leaves coming off sets of branches
Pterodactyl bones, x-rays
Of a fin, or a hand, or a wing

From the bones, come coin-sized
Leaves in layers to the white blank sky
Shivering in deference to the breeze

This is a love poem

The heart of one who loves shivers
In the same way those leaves do

Trembling in a silhouette
Against nothing

Transition

I guess now, she will have those men
Those good-looking ones, with
Pressed pants, and clean cars

Seeing me, she will recall other things
But surely, she has returned
To good-looking ones now

A Hole in the Sky

There is a hole in the sky

The sea washed the sand
Rhythmically and sensually
It will never cease that massage

I walked at the boundary
Of the land and sea
Beckoned forward

By the hole in the sky

My arms felt as though
Puppet strings called them
To throw, like a round ball

Everything into it
Particularly those things
Which grieve me

I suddenly came to know
That the hole in the sky
Was also calling for me

Someday I'll fly through it
Drawn upward on puppet strings

And be gone

Left Lane

This is the speed of things
At 6:40 a.m. the bay is silvered
The ferry came across, seemingly
For me alone
While on the other shore
I had to drive, for hours

I was born into beauty
I was handed beauty

Cities become dreams over my shoulders
Tank trucks become duellists

Broken, grey buildings
Are spotted with sunlight

Born into beauty, but
Temporarily had to run,
And so began running.

Why? I don't know.

I really do not know why.

To Women

We're supposed to want them
We're supposed to want them panting, cumming
We're supposed to want to buy them things
Build them homes
We're supposed to yearn for them
We're supposed to imagine them stretched before us
We're supposed to pledge to them
We're supposed to look at their exquisite bodies
We're supposed to share with them
We're supposed to dream of being with them, inside them
Tangle and turn them upside down
And make them scream, pull their hair

They are not the same as us
They are curved in the sunshine in a certain way
Their breasts, their hips, their asses are supposed
To tempt the abandonment of reason to
The animal

And their faces, eyes particularly
To tempt the superhuman

The World

Some say the world is merciful

They point to shaded patches of grass
Where we sit, beside flowing water
They point to the fruit trees, bearing gifts
They point to a breeze blowing across your lover's body

Some say the world is merciless

They point to men rotting in alleys
Ground under
They point to mothers grieving dead sons
Mutilated on the steppes, and to betrayal

But I say:

The mercilessness of the world
Can be merciful, like a cool cloth during fever

The mercy of the world
Can be merciless, like cold steel cutting a tumor

That's a bit of what they say
And a bit of what I say

What do you say?

In the Slaughterhouse

I came into this slaughterhouse
To walk a narrow line, to speak the truth
And to utterly refuse
To shirk the opening of the heart

In this brutal killing ground
Men and women are broken daily
Scattered by the wind, broken
Ground into cowardice and into abandoning

What they know is right

But this I will never do

In this dark cave of foolish lies
Where a man will sell his brother for an extra day
Or for a profit, or for pussy
I was unwillingly deposited one day

44 years ago

So watch. I won't give in.
And I won't take the easy road.

Watch.

Rolling Up His Sleeves

He was rolling up his sleeves
While he did this, carefully
He raised his eyes to the sky

He was going in, out of duty
Or out of blindness
Clarity, or ignorance

There was a small cloud
Obscuring part of the moon
A tiny bird across it

Flitting and darting
Chasing anything, something
Through the night sky

He saw the bird
He rolled his sleeves up,
And stepped

Over the threshold

At the Monument

Twirling on marble – studying
Arts martial
Receiving kind words from Tennessee

At the monument for the Union armies
Who fought against Tennessee

Reading the names of the generals
Reading the names of the units
And thinking of men, moaning and bloating
Blown in two by cannon

Fighting Tennessee
Calling out for the mothers, dying
Against Tennessee

While receiving, as I twirled
Studying martial arts

The kindest words I have ever heard
Coming from Tennessee

inside

the birds hopped from branch to curling branch
and he stepped inside his home

stepping inside his home, he found
the birds hopping from branch to curling branch

and he stepped inside his home
and there were the birds on the branches

through the gateway, through the door
into the place where the birds were hopping

from one branch to another, stepping
into his home to find that the birds were hopping

Goodbye

I don't want to say goodbye to you
But I guess I have to so this is it
I'm going to say goodbye now
Maybe someday I will see you

Now, after I say goodbye to you
I'll have to take a very long walk

For a very long time

never

i never wrote a poem
before i wrote this one
thanks very much
for reading this poem
i never wrote one
before this
so this is the first poem
i ever wrote

thanks

thanks for reading my poem
wherever you are and whoever you are
you took the time
to read my poem
i am glad you are there
i am glad you are reading this poem

and i want to thank you

i miss L

and i wish i would see her on the street
and then she would come towards me
and we would meet, like in my dreams

i really miss her right now
because this is her town
this is not my town, this is her town
this is not my world
this world belongs to L

i don't know where you might find
a world for me

new poems

these new poems are not the same
as any of the old ones
i really miss L
when we made love
i can't even speak about it
but i remember it very well
making love with her
for many hours at night before sleeping
L was once with me
and i remember lying
close to her

when i see

a beautiful woman or a white car
i think of L
with whom i shared a year and a half of life

i miss her – my best friend
i was able to talk to her really
about anything at all

now she's not here anymore
i didn't even see her today

the man she now makes love with
is not from this town

he is from another place
and that is where she goes now

L

L come here
please
im alone in this apartment
come here please

but you wont be coming here tonight
because you are driving
to sleep with your new boyfriend

so you wont be here tonight

never

ill never again make love with L

and i'll never again write a poem
like the poems i have written before about L
i'll never again lie with her and watch her move with me
i'll never be able to do that again
and there are some ways of writing poems
that i won;t be able to do again

i can see her body moving as i insist it moves
as though it was some dream

from which i had to awaken

this poem

this poem is not good
because it doesn;t say what i want to say

about what i learned today

Who Gives a Shit About the Way of the Samurai

Above all, when the enemy is scattered and disorganized, you must...

Hey! Wait!

Who gives a fuck about the Way of the Samurai

You dumbass arrogant fucks, get a life and stop killing people.

Ascendant

Now the eyes that were inside
Are outside
The imploring eyes
The quizzical eyes
The kind eyes

Have risen high into the sky
And now the eyes are in the clouds

Those eyes have become
The eyes of the entire World

Turning

The birds are wheeling and turning for you
Conspiring to center into you – you at the center of the circle
In the image, the jets wheel inward on a circle to you
They fight for you, the men obey your commands

Troopers converge on a target, in a spiral
You move in with them to make a kill
Seeing the flames silhouette a running man
And knowing that all of this vast galactic turning

Is for you, in you, and at your command
You close your fist with the lust of mastery
Then open it to release the dove of a new world

The Wasteland

They came in low over the cratered hills
And released their munitions
Flew screaming past in a glimpse
Of light, sun, and metal

Hours later, I picked my way through the ruins
Of this more contemporary wasteland

There was no flourish here
There was no linguistic self importance
Masking impotence

There were simply steps
And people checking into motels for sex
And children being ushered into empty rooms

In the Wasteland

Number One

They call me
I was standing in the stream
There were stones, and water flowing by them
I was asking

Where are you, my number one? Where are you?

You whom I adore
For whom I fight
and
For whom my tears flow

Last night in a dream – I went Mad for you

Where are you, my number one?

They are calling me back
But I am standing in the stream
My hand is clutching for you
To hold yours, the hand

Of my number one

The unearned things are going
The unearned thoughts are going

But the heart's desire remains.

no words

there is a deep river
running underground

it's the river of sorrow
and it runs
under the ground

everyone who has ever
will ever
cry a tear

has watered this river

there can be no more tears
there can be no fewer tears

and now
on this underground river
i have set sail

with no known destination

can you

can you tell when the next cloud will disappear?
can you count the drops in the sea?
can you number the blades of grass
on the sweeping prairie
or the dimensions of your lover's thought?

can you box regret?
can you chain the sky?
can you sit in the core of the earth?
can you breathe the vacuum?

can you collect the petal of a flower
and simultaneously keep it alive?

can you really tell me
why she is no longer beside me

or when these tears will cease?

The Coming Storm

If you watch for the signs of the animals
You'll see them, quivering, eyes to the sky
Turning to their burrows, turning to their dens
In a darkening afternoon – listen
As a hoof stomps nervously, and to the grasses rustling
As the herds swing through narrow canyons
To places more familiar

And men also, and women
Whose worlds are at the same time more wide
And more narrow than those of animals
Some of them are also picking up their faces
To the tired sky, out of their common dream
To the greying horizon where night now stands in
The core of midday – so in silent places

Where antennae quiver you can hear a dark-haired
Woman lean to speak with an angular man

She says to him: "there is a storm coming"
He, nodding, saying nothing

While they turn for shelter.

The Theater

I wonder who it is
That is tearing off that one's mask right now
And who is it
Who is putting the mask on the other one?

There are entire communities
Whose masks are being torn from them
And other nationalities
Who are putting them on

A sea of pale faces
And glittering eyes behind them

Dogs and Men

Main street: noisy, dirty, close, hot

Dogs circling, sniffing crotches

Some under awnings
incapable without coffee. And also
Incapable with coffee

Women passing by

The teacher who was with the woodworker
Was walking with a wide-hipped late summer
Fucker

The builder who has snowmobiles
Is now fucking the woodworker

Instead of his wife

Late summer on Main Street
Hot, dirty, cheap, and transient

Come looking for dogs
You will lack nothing

Come seeking a man

And you may leave disappointed

Mentally Ill Men and Young Women

Two mentally ill men smoking cigarettes
On the corner by subsidized housing
Near the crosswalk

One young woman crossing
With a bag from the food co-op
Halfway between curbs

Brutal rape, coitus interruptus,
martyrdom on the cross

Or an indifferent glance?

In 7 seconds we'll know.

The Secret

Someone tell me the secret
Of how to love another
When you have left them
Or they have left you

We are all already gone
All of this, is already gone

How do you do anything at all?

Now

I thought I was lost before
Now I know I am

I thought I knew grief before
But I did not

You can cast a thin line in the ocean
And fish for a great whale

You can leap from the top of a hill
Countless times, trying to touch the moon

You can skate across vast frozen lakes
With a can of juice and a snack

But you cannot correct foolish errors

And when someone really goes
Nothing in the Universe
No power in Eternity

Will ever bring them back.

Grief

They will pass it by
They will lay down quickly
Or smoke
They will drink, screw, watch television

And leave you to bear it.

The Light of Death

There is a light streaming
From emptiness

Streaming across us
Pouring over my face

Will you take my hand
And step out, into emptiness?

I was watching You
Like some speeding vessel

Passing by your own sound waves
Into the land

Where you can no longer hear yourself
All Sound

Is left behind

And now, You fly alone
You are moving beyond all sound

You have let loose my hand
And are streaming towards emptiness

Love and War

Nations in diplomatic interactions
Are smiling and handshaking
Sometimes grinning

But in the background
They assemble weapons
Maneuver armies

So they are showing the face of peace
But their actions betray them

Men and women in the public sphere
Are smiling and handshaking
Sometimes grinning

But in the silence of the mind
They are sucking, fucking
Moving in, moving out, leaving

So they are showing the face of decorum
But the Truth betrays them

Nightfall

So now night has fallen
The day is over
And your work is done

Tomorrow will require
Other things
And there will be other things to do

In the thread of a day
It may be possible
To hear a whispering logic

Of direction
But to hear it and to act upon it
Are two distinct things

Tomorrow there will be an opportunity
To take up your burden
And act upon it

The Last Night of Nocturne

And what is the significance of This?
And why is it that we do This?
For when, heads down, in the rain
We hear the recession of an endless train
And know that the empty tracks will so soon want
The heavy comfort of wheels again
So why is It done?
And why is it completed?
For when, heads down, they leave in the rain
For home and hearth, for pleasure
For work, for life and death
What is it they carry, and what retain?
And what is the reason, the reason we did this?
Your reasons are yours, and mine are mine
If reasons there are, if reasons you find
As for me, into the soaring night it flies
To eternity, upwards in the wet-drenched skies
I know that on the narrow track of the future
No significant answer will be found
And in the echoing caverns of the past
Mere clues, mere trails scratched in hollow ground
So I go, on the curving upward bending street
Beneath a ceaseless, steady rain
Under the beat, of the Heart of the world
And its bittersweet, ephemeral kiss
It was not for then, not even for now
But it might have been for This

The Eastern Front

Two Madmen Were Beaten

Beaten badly
Can you see them?
More importantly
Can you feel them?

And so at Kursk tankers were burnt to death
Screaming within iron tombs

And at Stalingrad
Men perished calling for their mothers
By the hundreds of thousands
Burnt with jellied gasoline
Shot by snipers
Frozen to death
Blown apart

In Leningrad
The bones froze solid
in a three year siege

Behind the lines
The SS herded jews
And tore the breasts off villagers
One by one
With combat knives

Can you feel the madmen who were beaten?
Just little children
When they were brutalized
They determined, both of them
Never again to be humiliated

Others paid for it

Who knows the dark grey green horror
At the bottom of the world?
Who can stop the tanks
When they begin to move?
Or the death ovens
When they warm to exterminate?

Jew? Russian? Nazi? Partisan? German soldier.
Child.

A child dead in the street.
A child picking through corpses.
A child on the last German lines in 45.
A child rushing through the Russian winter night.
A little girl raped, by whom?

And does it matter? Because the rapes, once started, never stop.

Who will stop it?

Will you?

Can you?

The World

It was just yesterday
When I let go the hand of a phantom
And saw light appearing through the window
Between curled branches

It was only yesterday
And photographs from the War
A German family dead: suicide
As the Russians entered Berlin

It was yesterday
In confession to a little priestess
A wild bitch-angel with a snug
Imaginary pussy – that

I came up against the walls
Inside myself

Me, the self-styled wielder
Of the jackhammer of the mind
Me, the one who scoffs
At walls others build to guard

Precious illusions

Found myself reduced to the great
Commonality, and infinitesimal –
Traversing the endless, arced, curving
Grey, impassive edifice

That I meticulously, assiduously
Built around my own Heart

The Dance

In the dance hall
One can see two lines

Here, by the banquet tables
The compromisers

There, by the stone doors
The unyielding

Note how the first group stands at ease
Well fed
And listen to them speak

But do not forget the second company
Lean, solitary
Who stand in silence

In this world
Of shadow and sunlight

You will always find them

The children of the flexible
Who dance, and make merry

On the graves of the rigid
Who died fulfilling

Oaths of protection

This Company

It looks as though
My time on this earth
Is coming to an end

How many days are left?

How many days of song
And of light and shadow?

It has been
A good company
That I have walked with

Strong hearts, brave faces
And true words

Some striking out at the darkness
Some passing through it

Some standing
Others falling on the Way

Now, I never thought
That I would stumble

But you see me
Staggering
By the stone gates

Friend, when you find me there
Won't you please
Stop a moment

And gently place a cool cloth
Across my brow

Before you pass me by?

The Sun

A horde of bicyclists moves towards the sun
In yellow vests, helmeted, mostly glasses, fast

And like some salmon spawning, I am out
Running in a different direction

The bicyclists are determined to get to work
Their faces squint, they avoid the direct glare

That is warming my back – I have nowhere to go

Later, when their souls are shielded by tinted glass
And high heels, when they lean forward quietly

That's my time to turn, to stop running
And walk step by step

Directly into the blinding sun.

Long Weekend

I saw several women yesterday and today
Several women, and girls
And I was wondering
When you broke those hearts
Which woman were you, across from your opponent
When you held the position of power and choice?
I saw someone sitting
Across from me, speaking sincerely
Who does not wish to be a trophy wife
And I saw your picture on the bookshelf
A girl, leaning on her elbows, and looking for
A good conversation, and if necessary,
a Frenchman for your bed
I felt your foot under the table,
And longed to enter your room last night
Your sleeping 7 feet from me
May have saved me in an inexplicable way
I also saw, on the stone steps, throwing acorns
Without glasses,
Extraordinary beauty under the trees
And today – when you lifted your arms
To hold your hair, to do something with your hair
And we agreed, to walk and to talk
I was dropped like a stone into deep green seas
Elevated as a feather in a mighty wind
Simultaneously
Still, you move and you assess
And from behind fashionable glasses
Even behind inquisitive eyes
You have become my ephemeral companion
For the passage through a narrow strait
Between the cliffs of Time and Desire
As you move, up and down the stairs
I feel the future like a wind
And see you playing with shells
In a dress, the breeze blowing
On the untouchable, unknown
Shores of childhood

The Experiment

You are going to do this too
Someday

How will you do this?

Soon, you may hear my knock
On your door

Soon, I may hold my hand to you
I may take your hand

And ask you to come away with me.

Thoughts

And what
If logic itself is true
But its window dressing
false?

If the prophets
Hand out coins
No longer acceptable
for commerce?

If the horizon
Of the mind
Is narrower
Than a pin?

If the pleasure seeker
Sinks his arrow
Into a very
Misleading target?

What then?

The Rose

What is the reason
For tending roses?

The flower
We know, will die

In the coming
Cold wind

And yet,
We tend them

On fields
Of ash and stone

Seeing
In our dreams

Fields of
Quivering flowers

Believing
That though our time

Is barren
There will be a day

When children
Will see these fields

Storm Passing

The sun appeared
An hour before I left
The island. I was sweeping
The sand through a trapdoor

But I could not resist
One more walk to the sea
So in the cold wind
I went up to the beach

There was a savage surf
Coming in sideways, whipped
With foam. Metal grey and roaring
Lapping at the dunes

This is not a sea for swimmers
Not even a sea for surfers
It is only a sea for two classes:

The despairing, or the professional

Before turning back, I spoke to the sea
Seeing two split-screen visions:
One: A man sailing, pulling up nets
Two: A man drowning, disappearing in the waves

Before turning, I spoke to the sea
And this is what I said:

"Not this time. Perhaps soon.
But not this time."

Him

Now I am walking with him
I consistently see his face
Looking up at me
He wears a Norwegian sweater

His hair is bowl cut
His eyes are eager
His hands hold a flower
Or he holds my hand

Now I am sitting with him
He looks out from inside me
He is hoping someday
That I will join him

A long time ago
The thing I call myself
Left the thing I call him
But he was all along

Coming behind, following
And I never saw him
So, now he has caught me

And I cannot be the same
Again

Dream

It was early morning, when light was
Just beginning to enter the room.

I heard a sound from outside.
The sound of tires on gravel.

I went to the window, opened the window.
It was you there, looking up.

Through those eyes of yours.
With that long red hair of yours.

You were calling my name, beckoning.
I dressed quickly, went down the stairs

Opened the door, breath frosting the air.
I walked to you, where you waited.

You took my hand.
We looked into one another's eyes.

(In yours I saw galaxies, and the world's end.)

You drove us away.
My hand rested on your leg.

We drove far from this land.
And passed through the gates of Eternity.

Autumnal

In the first storms of autumn
Leaves are being torn from the trees
Like tears when someone wails with grief

They pour off in wild sheets, the trees
Turn and yield them – some breaking
Lying, shattered and sideways after the gale

After that there is a peace

One sees through branches to a crystal sky
But a few leaves tremble before the
First snowfall, analogous to stubborn
Memories and closeted hopes

Reluctantly falling alone, one by one

Until the winter, when the metallic sky
Surrounds every branch

A discerning eye will catch
The one or two leaves remaining
Unwilling to fall, not giving up

Like an old man's memories of Love

Beloved

Behold, she has stopped my tongue.

Behold, she who comes in blazing beauty.

Behold, my beloved cometh out
And she passeth beneath the trees.

Yes, she comes, my beloved.
I call for her, and she comes.

Now the ancient lands can
Let loose their firm hold
And sink into the sea.

Now fountains and rivers can
Sing their songs of joy.

My beloved has now come to me.

Shells

Your long fingers are curled underneath the collar
Of my overcoat

And crabs are doing whatever
They must do to loosen their shells

In preparation for an exposed
Scuttle beneath the waves

I sense you are about to peel the shoulders
Of the coat back, and help me

Slip my arms out

While serpents, in darkness
Metabolize swallowed mice, loosening the translucent skin

That once glowed upon them

You undo the buckles of my armor
Your hands find my body

The world sighs, seeking release from
What once covered it

And now you reach into me
And peel off the dead skin

Of my former life.

Rest

Night used to be a cloak
To cover the things
He did not want the Sun to see

Then the darkness
Became a wrap
To rest his eyes
From the light of day

Now it's different

Because the beauty
Of her presence is brilliant
The eyes of his soul
Have further opened

To the Sun that shines
Behind the former sun

Now sleep comes easy
When he knows
Her beauty preceded
And will follow it

One cannot stare at Her too long
Just like the sun

Mute

It's a grey day

The interior lights
Are reflected in the cup

The music speaks
Of solitude

While the windows show
The black branches

When you put away
Your cup and teapot

You can step outside
Where everyone,

and everything

Is covered
By the grey sky

spring – for minnesota

park comes up through city
scent the open grasslands

empty vistas
lakes and ponds

shine silver fluttering vibration
upward into the eye

a mirror with a searchlight behind

beside the shimmering water
disappear into the Spring

the heart and its longings
rising and flooding time

with its needs

disappearing into spring
by glittering pools

and floating away

on currents of clear desire

minnesota 1

walking at right angles
to ten thousand mirrors

walking into a sky
the color of steel

walking through two planes
into fifteen

walking on into emptiness

ambition

under an entirely subtle
and painted sky

and before 7
the jets appear lazy
arcing in lines

rising

one by one to destinations
seeming not-too-distant
from eternity

and i

who used to run
the stadium in Hanover
for the inimitable pleasure
of sweet, sweet pain

am running the long, long steps
rising, then loosely
descending the grasses

to climb again

and so i climb again
and again
and the jets climb
again, and again

and that sweet, sweet pleasure
no one

can take from the travelers
from the pilots
from the sky
from the jets

or from me

calling

now you are back in the hospital
and your mind is spinning out crystalline trails
vainly making sense of past nonsense

you, a black-haired dream
may take my hand this summer

and i will be your strong armor

we will feel the cool sand

between our toes while we wait
for whomever summons us
when it is time to go

When they tell you this and that

When they tell you about this and that
Don't buy into it at all

and in some way I do not know
This is related to why

right now
I cannot cry

that little dumpling said to me
"you again"

and then chose not to do it this time
so i'll have to work with her again

next time

don't buy into building any castles by the shore
or ladders to the clouds

id rather do it with you tonight
but if we cannot

i'll be forced to do it with you

in another body
and on another world

at some other time

Good Night

Good night
My sweet ones
Good night

Now it is time
To turn out the light

I will protect you
I'll not let you come
To any harm

The world is large
Larger than we know
My sweet ones

When you sleep
You will float

Through the canyons
Of this world

And pass into the blue beyond

So good night

Phase

Dragonfly : dissolution

Waterfowl : peripheral

Woman : beckoning

Sky : everywhere

The Speed of Sound

she speaks of reich speaking about porn
and then breaks into a child or animal's sounds

whereas i hypothesize my nose behind her ear
and we luminously gather anything that any star has left

can you watch us now, gathering speed?
like stanley kubrick, like the best athletes, like beethoven

like an asteroid just barely missing the sun
so getting shot back out even faster into the icy void

im taking a down escalator, somehow standing tall against the scourge
of invisible whips – coming down the escalator

she – passing in the opposite row, in dark
the object of predating male .... whatever

pass me a cup of tea, sit with me in some french quarter
let the world spin, let people work, let them toil

let them lie, and let us lay down

Day and Night

Do not let your left hand know
what your right hand is doing.

And if you ride on surface coverings
Then ride smoothly my friends, and be sure
To ride grandly, ride far and fast
Smiling, letting the sun glint off your white teeth

Pray unto thy father in secret chambers
do not make a show of it.

And if you decide to pick moon fruits
Wandering through floating world print gardens
Licking on stamp books of Yoshitoshi
And eating the heads of enemies, the genitals of women

Before the cock crows
you will have denied me three times

Walking beside alpine pools
Pausing to drink clear water
Unfurling sail, or pulling it in
As the time, the wind, and the sea require

Why, oh why
hast thou forsaken me?

She sits on you, she bites you
She crawls on top of you, the drapes gently
blow in the black breezes
And you cry out, and you finally tell the whole truth

It is accomplished.

aristocracy

You sense behind you
an irresistible buildup

A nameless, insatiable
demand for breakthrough

An eternity of beauty
rushes through you

You have inherited vast fortunes
and their attendant responsibilities

You hold on to all this
as though the very world
was waiting for you

You say:

Of the dull, what is required
is not what is required
of those who shine

But:

How long
can you hold on?

in a tower

a man in a tower
is reading
by the light of a candle
what he is reading

i don't know

i do not know at all

is it a guidebook
to the masonry
or a map to the view
from the window?

i will never know

in the meantime
outside
the sun shines
the seasons change

the storms come and go

The World's End

where earth rivers pour out into the void
thought to be at the edges of a flat planet
are here on the unswept streets

these rivers appear to me, and to no one else
to be sweeping the avenues
to be rushing through the alleys
as wilderness canyons

when they swell and pour
over the edge of time
they freeze in the reaches of space

amidst shreds of yesterday's plastic
and the wind whipping of Islamic fabric
the playing of children, the swaying of trees
and the thoughtless drone of traffic

it seems that no one else
hears these waters move

Other Poets

At the seashore
Some kids throw stones
Others take their rafts or boogie boards way out
Some collect stones and shells
Some lie in the warm sand near the dunes
Their spirits silhouetted against the sea

In the forest
Some birds warble, others trill, others crow
Little animals scamper around
Bigger ones rustle or stay still
While we come walking through
With the kids ahead

All under the shelter of the trees

Stone

She held the stone outside that sculptor's dwelling
It was her own and solitary: "Gates of Hell"
The child of her desire for copulation/his rejection thereof
Who is greater, she or he? Rodin is august,

But what of her experience on the outside of his radius?

And in a square chamber Kollwitz helps us
Also become a stone or metal mother wrapped around
That which is most precious to her: who can bear it?
Although it is stone or metal alone.

I'd like to curl on her doorway just like a mistress.

I am the mother of the stillborn child of my love.

Ruins

Have you ruined me for all others?
I do think you have

There is a sheet of plexiglass
On one side, my past
My dreams, my naivete, and you

On another side, my now
My waking moments, and my decay

Your net has captured analogues,
Ancillary loves, places
Sand and sea

Time itself is strung through your funnel

Typhoon

Today is for studying the Beaufort Scale
For understanding rescue
In the breeches buoy formed by the
Wonderful curve between the shoulder blades
Of three women at the bookstore

Or to tell a friend that the story began
When Macwhirr tapped the barometer

The foamy swells of time are whipping white
Froth by me and warning flags snapping
In high strung wires as irresistible green seas
Wash across the decks on Cleveland Avenue

When she smiled at me I heard

Hatchbolts, even keelbolts
Beginning to give way

Falling Away

The source of value is arcing back in on itself
Arrows are disobeying common sense
Returning to bows.

I have only a toe left inside the dance
Of the sleepwalkers
But the irony is in the cast iron nature of life.

As I exit this cage, and leave the gruntings behind
The shell that surrounds me
Grunts more boldly than ever.

In Traffic

you have to understand
the two variable play of music and traffic

so for example
at times you may be travelling faster than the traffic
and for that reason
in conjunction with some song that drips power
you may believe yourself

superhuman

and then in another time
with ice sheeting the roads
and quiet baroque, so as to be able
to hear the environment and its hazards
you consider yourself

prudent

or in summer
with something haunting and heartbroken playing
and left lane acceleration because the ease is right
so you have further to travel
and everyone is going at the same rate
the sun glints off cars
you consider yourself

content

nD

canst thou reach in and cup that pure rose dwelling beneath my ribs?
in spite of antipathy to poesie anglaise

so in diversion from that hallowed tradition and with respect
to the ongoing ravel-shostakovich dialogue

let this then be as much a glittering thing that sparkles unexpectedly
from the void and then as easily transfigures (this poem, not THIS)

the rose that is pointed to by Jesus is trembling
some roses must grow upside down, and flower
(at least for a time) in the cool ground

your fingers are holding it

The Tiger (to Blake and Stevens equally)

The tiger was moving by the fence
Then the tiger sat down on the rock
From the balcony the children watched the tiger
And it started to roar, and roar
Not loud, not quietly, by the fence

Just as though saying
I am beyond weary of this pen
I deserve better than this pen

How to put this?

The world was surrounding the tiger
The tiger was blowing the world
Into bits

I'll never see anything
In the same way again

Fields

The world is a strange field upon which deeds are written
An interlaced web of mirrors in which faces are revealed

Deeds of courage send perturbations out through these fields
And also thoughts which seem to be wired in between everything

What good are miracles to those of us left behind
Are they any better than lighthouses to ships already wracked on the reefs?

This field and its events are not two
Existence precedes essence

These deeds turn brushes that paint colors on wheels that spin back
Upon themselves over eternity

The Lattice

In inky blackness or across paper thin surfaces
You could call them the opposite of cracks appearing
Invisible to the eye
On a non-liquid through which constantly travel
Waves of truth

Outside of your toes, of your eyes, of that facial expression, of your nails
Wrapped around the phallus of my ego and not roughly moving

Beautiful

No one should prod or poke this eternal surface in its congealing
For these you must know are the opposite of cracks

Fun

You cannot prod or poke it you must let it stand and you must let the opposite of cracks
Like the fingers of trees on a steel sky or light on light in thousands of lights
Or nerves, or dancing organisms, dancing – do not prod them

You must say "beyond good and evil" which is the same as a code word for
truth

If you want to keep your love – kiss

Do not under any circumstances let either fear or haste touch these gradually appearing
Opposites of cracks because these lines
Are a painting

of Love

Bombings

You go back and forth

What you do to them
What they do to you

Your retribution
For what they did to you
Strengthens them
Their strength

Strengthens you

You never crush one another

You do, however

Crush those of us who take off
The armor

You do, however

Succeed in killing gentleness

With your vests and backpacks
With your guns and helicopters
And sports sunglasses

You won't kill them
But you will trample us

D.B.

You had a sense of something beyond the horizon
The small victories of commerce could not satisfy you
And this because there is a final Victory
Beyond the splashings of boys with toy boats
Well beyond the nervous struggle for a small advantage

It no longer was a matter of the theft of another's items
Or utterance of words, even one's own

I came to know you this evening
Waves dashed up, silvery, against stone
All was monotone save for some edge of the sky
Where a light, where a color, hovered in almost
Consciousness of its own delicacy
Against the gloom

It is my belief
That your action was designed not for this sandbox struggle
This grimacing and grunting for a flag
But rather
For that sole strip at the edge of the world
Between the clouds

Sailing

the bay thawed
you walked by its border
and into its rippling surface you stared

knowing that dry land
was the place of lies and commerce

the bay is enclosed
on one side by large homes
satisfied people on a thin strip between waters
on the other by the vast cathedrals of industry
grain, metal, ore, ships, fire, energy

you looked to the bridge and it came to you
this indistinct line on the other side
the very tip of an ancient hollow
thousands and thousands and thousands
of gallons of water, fresh water

lost in its center dying of hunger
one would not die of thirst

itself dwarfed by seas of silence
seas of blue and coral
seas of wild storms and ice
seas of windless haze for miles

where you had premonitions of death
and you wondered how you would accept it
how would you go to it when it came
so many many days from a quiet sunlit street

early days of spring
no white sails yet moving on the
shattered surface

the bay
can be contained by the lake
the lake
can be contained by the seas
the seas

are only contained by One Thing

Sappho/Priests

Walking by the water longing – at the same time exploring the contours of the longing.

Desired bodies moving in the trees – the hand has a memory or a premonition, or both, of a curve and a resistance.

Zoroastrians tending fire in some fabric, which is blown by the wind cutting through the crags.

Catholic priests at the pizzeria seated in a booth, leaning slightly forward.

Their voices low and propagating into the shadows until the next Order arrives.

Dreams

To stay in a place where the dreams of the night like yellow arrows on some diagram of war or penetration can percolate into the activities of the day is suchwise a choice to begin to present the totality of a strange sphere to these blocked grids that once made up an incomplete picture of what was to be during the sunlight.

The penetration can be sideways or you might force it downwards. In which case the analogy which is under consideration sort of like a plastic sheet with a few colored lines laid over something is one of mining and therefore you're after gems and jewels and suchlike things that you value. Or just to lay back and open up and allow it on you won't discard anything that injects you – or to think of it in horizontal dimensions bubbling upwards and wondering standing by the caldera or the geyser or whatever kind of hole in the earth just what may come oozing or blasting up this time.

The day makes love to the night and in so doing finds a way to break beyond its stubborn, unsatisfactory constraints. The night copulates with the day because it wishes to be known. It does not wish to be always alone.

Children's artwork. Foreign cities.

The premonitions of new worlds.

Submission

There were tips and underwater portions

What matters in the choices is more the latter

I imagined that you were in need

Dreamt that I breathed life into you

From a statue to a moving thing

Then assumed that your breath, reciprocally, turned me to stone

The Master of Ch'an

In any field of vision one finds seduction which can take the form of a structure that begs the eye to fall on certain positions, colours, what have you, forms and yet on for example a daily walk in which the he had noted earlier fronds of palms swinging above were akin to the pom-poms of lanky cheerleaders but do not be confused for the thing which was you might say not penetrated by the world penetrating iron needle nor caught in the bubbling net was not the sky, nor wasn't it

He had for some time swum in a spun yarn tale which always looked or told itself that it looked between things and in that long hallway that was a reminder of some past movie treating the future he asked himself then if you step beyond that particular fiction just like stepping around this corner and pulling out that set of keys you might find your whatever that thing should not be called thrust minus propulsion into whatever it was doing and be enabled to exit the monastery gate

the coat of wintertime

put the coat of wintertime on me – put the long dark heavy coat of wintertime on me –
you are putting the cloak of wintertime on me

i am shouldering the long dark cloak of wintertime

buttoning, buttoning, buttoning up

for the march into the distant snow-covered mountains

the hammer falls

the distant beating of the hammer can now be heard

with a thud – a thud – and not with a word

the hammer is coming and the hammer has struck

like night, like cold, like the distant beat of a drum

you have been struck, i have been struck, by this cold metal heavy hammer

beating out the marching sound of time on the human heart

it comes when darkness drops down and when the cloud layer is low

and when the pages of books blacken not with fire but with disinterested readers

all is not lost, however, for what does it mean to be beaten down by this hammer?

it merely means to suffer the same defeat as all the others do

walking stooped, dancing wildly, standing alone

listening to the beat of far distant drums

collection

do not rise too quickly for there is a collection to be made

and brought into the sunshine

last night: i drove, and in the back seat, a lovely slender woman in a dress

who suffered. I recall reaching back to take her hand, our hands met and held

in that which has meant comfort and kindness for all time

so do not rise too quickly for there is a collection to be made

gather quietly that which was spoken from the unknown place

in the silent night

that

it is the thing which prompted the utterances of the norwegian resistance fighter and later the nervousness of the munitions coordinator who saw the print that was made by the sculptor and it is the thing in her sculpture of the woman holding the dead child and the very same thing bending the trees today

on the autumn walk amongst the barren branches

Inheritance

It has a logic and a command if one listens for it.

At a certain point, after a sustained inbreath.

One may come to this conclusion: i will take this all out to its end point and i will not shrink from the implications of it

here is where one must be willing to _____

and that is all

the stream

how does a stream or a fountain save a life?

it may reach for you as you stand on the bridge

or you may reach for it – then

walk to sit on the stones by the fountain

and drink water from the bottle you are carrying

the end of the game

the game is over

it's not a loss or victory

it's that the game is done, concluded

there will not be another

you can hold a banner

the sounds of the crowd ringing

a low chant that moves again and again

down time's pale narrow hallway

the red bridge

in the morning

out usually

the sun flamed in red on the iron struts of the bridge

and it was as though that never-seen sight

for just that minute

opened a gate into worlds beyond

the town of disappearance

quiet apartments

former lovers, executives, criminals, politicians, professors

on the sun-dried, cracked sidewalks

stopping in shops, thrift stores, florists, libraries

shielding their faces from the bright light

The Solution for Heartbreak

The solution for heartbreak is to

Become nothing

The solution for heartbreak is to enter oblivion

The solution for heartbreak

Is to agree to be buried alive

Must one elaborate?

The problems with heartbreak are the protests, the cries

The problem is the disbelief

And the solution is simply

To lie down and be broken finally

You are the Rock

upon which i was defeated

the grey horde of ambition swollen

parting on your edge – your victory

running full-speed into your scalpel

so the skin of my heart gets unfolded

by the true and real tutor of mortality

you – the form of mortality –

instructrix in oblivion

that smile you gave me

when we parted the final time

what exactly was it?

a playground child, on the way after recess

the game over

you have the marbles in your beautiful, closed fist

Attrition

lately i was down to a sort of layered paper that i was able to lay over things

down from concretized stuff to the interpretation of things and the painting in the colours of affect

which made of a moment, a work of art and allowed for a sort of investment in narcissism, or a bit better an infusion of pleasure and self interest and self respect and self

yes

the trees on both sides of the road have become familiar

I am down to this:

a car, the music in the car, the lens over the car and the music in the car and

no more significance

Alexander P. Gutterman was born in 1964 in New York City. He graduated from Stuyvesant High School, earned a philosophy degree from Dartmouth, and later attended the University of California, Davis, where he obtained a master's degree in philosophy. After intervals in California and New England, he lived in Minnesota for eleven years. During this time he earned a master's degree in counseling psychology.

In 2021, he moved to Colorado, where he now works as a therapist. Between 2013 and 2021, he wrote, directed, and produced several film projects, including the features *In Winter* and *The Hunter*. Alex continues to be actively engaged in the arts, primarily in poetry and film.

www.ingramcontent.com/pod-product-compliance
Lightning Source LLC
Chambersburg PA
CBHW072006090426
42740CB00011B/2117